Flying Free

By Sarah Colina

"Dedicated to my mother Janet Winifred Timms, who has believed in me all my life. Thank you."

Front cover original artwork by Sarah Colina.

Foreword

This collection of poems by Sarah Colina arrives at a poignant crossroads. Here, within these pages, lies not just a testament to a singular voice, but a final, vibrant echo from a life nearing its close. Sarah Colina, a poet whose brilliance remained largely unseen until now, offers us a remarkable gift: a glimpse into the depths of her psyche.

The poems themselves stand unveiled, raw and unfiltered. They speak of experiences both universal and deeply personal, inviting us to share in Sarah's joys, sorrows, and profound observations on the human condition. It's a testament to the power of her art that these poems resonate with such clarity, even without the usual context of a literary life fully lived.

Within these pages you will find an abundance of pain, yet underneath it all: bravery; the poet lays bare her vulnerabilities with unflinching honesty, inviting readers to share in the complexity of her experience. Her poems are a proof to the transformative power of courage and vulnerability, offering solace and inspiration to those who dare to delve into the depths of their own emotions.

One can't help but also sense a quiet urgency in these verses. Perhaps it's the knowledge of her own mortality that imbues each line with a heightened intensity. Yet, there's also a celebration of life here, a fervent grasp at beauty amidst the transient.

As you delve into Sarah's words, let them transport you. Imagine them penned not just with ink, but with the very essence of a life about to conclude. Here lies the power of her poetry – a testament to the enduring spirit, the unwavering pursuit of expression even in the face of finality.

This discovery of Sarah's work is a bittersweet one. We celebrate the unearthing of a hidden talent yet mourn the circumstances surrounding its unveiling. However, let her voice be a reminder: the human spirit's capacity for creation is boundless, and the power of words can transcend all limitations, even mortality itself.

Katy Streets

Just for a Moment

I was riding through the sky
on storms of doubt and fear,
when I hitched a lift upon your cloud,
floating gently so near.

Lost myself for a moment
that I knew would never last,
but I'll always see that part of me
when I smile in a looking glass.

Ode to a Friend

Ode to a friend without heart or vein,
ode to our castle, our little domain.
Liz may squeal and Daniel shout,
Dad will argue and Steven pout.
The dogs have growled, and the cat meow
and Mum and I have had a row,
but in this house, we've seen it all,
it's watched us rise and it's seen us fall.
The parties that raised its leaking roof and the door that
hid the pains and the truth.

It's had its share of pets galore,
from those that squeak to those that roar,
it's often been nicknamed Noah's ark,
the gardens resembled a national park.
Nappies and rompers have swung on its lines whilst the
carpet accepted the crumbs and the wine.

The remnants of childhood still linger there, the family
loyalty and mutual care,
so as you lock it's faithful old door,
into its chambers to enter no more,
Remember the house where we all grew,
as you lock out the old and open the new.

On the Breeze of Time

When you died, I thought my life
had come to a sudden end,
for in your parting I had lost
my Granny and my friend,
but now I realise
that though you are not here,
your presence and your soul will be forever near.

So, fly my Granny, on the breeze of time,
to the top of the mountains you can climb,
to the ends of the earth you may roam,
for eternity's your time-piece
and the clouds your home.

And in our hearts for all time you'll remain,
though our souls may grow heavy,
and spirits may wane.
Now "I love you Gran" is all there's left to say,
and I'll see you again some brighter day.

Come on, Grandads Dream!

Grandad, I remember the times we'd have a bet,
then off to the pub for a game of pool we'd set.
Two or three beers later with a shot or two to end,
we'd go back to watch the races,
two slightly drunken friends.
Dream about the lottery and owning our own horse, the name
that we would give him cos he would win of course!

So one day at Ascot, if I can you'll hear me scream.....
"He may be a flat horse but COME ON Granddads Dream!"

Lost

"What do I want from this world?"
Cries the lonely lady in black,
"How far from my routes have I wandered?
Is there no chance to ever go back?
All of my dreams are now ended,
like me they are empty and spent.
I once had it all in the palm of my hand,
can you tell me, where it all went?"
Then she weeps icy tears that trickle
and fall down the craggy lost old face,
and with nothing but memories left in this world,
says farewell to the human race.

The Id

I dream of being more than I can ever be
for I believe that somewhere
there must be another me,
living life for all it has to offer you and I,
knowing all the loving
but she'll never have to die,
my Id will always conquer
the world in which we live,
giving all to man
that one woman has to give.
Making all the promises,
living all the dares,
being all the woman
without any of her cares.
Bleeding hearts and sacrifices
have no place to dwell
with the woman who knows nothing
of our heaven or our hell.

Fairies and Elves and Pixie Glens

In a time now past for ever more,
behind a stately deep blue door,
there played two children, girl and boy,
with souls of laughter, hearts of joy.
Their time of childhood now has past
as taller shadows in life they cast,
but they still remember with fondness and cheers
those past yet not forgotten years,
of Fairies and Elves and Pixie Glens,
of passwords and secrets and magical dens,
the games and the stories, the trips to the sea,
the times when they knew how to laugh and be free.

Now the boy is a man, and the girl is a wife,
and they've both learnt to feel
the sharp edge of the knife.
They've left all their Santa's in sacks by the bed
and all of their fairies have long since fled,
but their family love will still remain
to see them through the storm clouds and rain,
for they'll never forget all the joy that they knew
behind the closed door of their home 212.

Gone but not Forgotten

Times move on, people change, things alter,
but we should never forget where we came from,
who we are.
Never forget their pains and their losses,
for a moment see life through their eyes...

Hear the bomb drop, see the child scream.
Would you know where shelter is?
Cold and frightened, hungry and alone.
When the siren stops where will you go?

So, as we live our comfortable lives,
free of poverty and tyranny,
remember the costs of our freedom,
the things we take for granted.

So don't mock the old lady as she shuffles by
or the gent who's forgotten his way,
just stop for a moment and thank them
for their part in our yesterdays.

The Puppet Master

With a word you stole all my tomorrows
and changed the pattern of my destiny,
only remembering the sorrow
you cast aside the joy you shared with me.

Threw my dreams upon the rocky shore
and stripped me of my pride,
when you said that you were mine no more,
my grief could find no place to hide.

So now I lie awake at night
with demons rushing through my head,
I have lost the will to fight
without you I breath, yet I am dead.

The light that shines ahead grows dim;
I find it hard to see the way.
My future prospects looking grim,
when all I want is yesterday!

Pretender

Twisting and turning in a world full of tears,
using bleaches and makeup to hold back the years,
dreaming that I'm still the girl I once was,
in charge of my life, I'm still my own boss.

Lost little soul, scared and alone,
When the lights go out the demons can roam,
Screaming and shouting, I'm losing my mind,
one day a corpse is all that they'll find.

She tried to be normal but didn't succeed.
She's not what we want, let alone what we need.
Poor epileptic she was really a fool,
a raving mad lunatic trying to act cool.

An Epileptics Tale

I have eyes long before I see,
hear your voice long before I speak.

Have the feeling although I cannot touch,
do not underestimate the soul that knows so much.

In a body that two worlds try to hold,
there's a halfway place where all the truth unfolds.

What you call affliction I call a gift divine,
for in those moments in between, all your words are mine.

Another World

You took me to another world that I had never seen,
taught me to believe in ways verging on obscene,
anarchy and freedom were the words you used to say,
family and loyalty to you was not the way.
Take my hand you told me, and I'll show you greater things,
freedom is the way that life begins.

But now I'm left with nothing
but the memory of those words
and the stark reality that every one was just absurd!

I had a Dream

I was given a dream, it was the best I ever had,
I let you share it, all you did was turn it bad.
Now I've a nightmare left to live it on my own,
where roses used to bloom only weeds have stayed and grown.

I had a secret place I chose to share with you,
you found another friend
with whom to share it too.
Now I am stranded with no place left to hide,
no secret getaway, no dream to hold inside.

Only sorrow dwells where my spirit used to live,
no fight or hope left, for you took all I had to give.
I had a dream but now the dream is through,
I once had laughter now all I have is YOU!

Just one of those Days!

When you get up in the morning
and there's toothpaste in the sink,
and the noise is so atrocious that
you can hardly think,
guess who got up before you!
The dog has had a hair cut
and his fur is in his bowl,
didn't my hydrangeas
once live in that large hole,
and who has had the glue?!
The list of dirty deeds is mounting up
and I haven't even finished my first cup.
Is this the start of things to come?
Who on earth would be a Mum?!
"I didn't mean to do it" a little voice proclaims,
"but if you want to know who did,
I'll gladly give you names!"
and then she simply stands there looking glum.
"How sweet she is," I hear them say
as we go to the shops,
"She's such a little darling, she really is the tops",
if only they knew!

The shopping spree is over
homeward bound at last,
but now the little darling phase has passed,
after all it was too good to be true.
No sooner are we through the door
then trouble strikes again,
first you hear the crash
and then the streaks of pain,
what will I find behind the door?
A wide-eyed cat streaks past my feet,
straight over a plate of half thawed meat,
and there's Lizzy on the floor,
"It was the cat, she did it, I never touched a thing",
different story but the same old ring,
and then she starts to cry...
"I was only trying to help you, I'll clean it up, OK?",
then hurries to the door to make her getaway,
all I can do is sigh.

Always

My life's been good, I'm sure of this,
warm summer nights, soft sultry kiss.
The long embraces, bodies entwined
union of both our souls and mind.
So, kiss me now with lips so warm
and be my shelter from the storm,
for if I do not see another night
I will not have left without a fight.

My love, my strength, my very breath,
you are the one card I have left,
the ace up my sleeve to save my soul,
the striker who'll score the final goal.

You've brought me love like I've never known
with you by my side I'm never on my own.
You're my strength, my lover, my special friend,
you took a heart in shatters and taught it to mend.
Gave my soul a chance, gave my spirit hope,
gave me reason to learn how to cope.

You showed me sympathy when I didn't know why
and lent me a shoulder when I needed to cry,
you bring me up when I feel down
by being my lover or being my clown.

Lost Smiles

I try to smile, instead my body cries,
I mean to laugh, but it comes out as a sigh
If I had strength I'd fight, but all has gone,
would vainly cling to love but there is none.
Each day is a trial until it's end,
where sometimes in my dreams I find a friend.

Fortune and good reason now have flown,
I pray for death whilst sitting on my own.
Befriended now by doubt and fear
and fading memories of brighter years,
when I was young and all lay bright ahead,
that I would be remembered when I am dead.

Silly thoughts of one so young and free,
but truth is now that all forget me,
and nothing makes the being born worthwhile,
and all that in between is but a trial.
So let this life end soon and I will cheer,
that I no longer need to face next year.

'Til facing New Year becomes a forgotten chance,
and all that's gone before a mere glance
of where the road could have led -
next year.

Over

There are times when the dream is over
and all the hope has turned to dust,
when the future has no meaning,
and you survive because you must.
The things you thought would keep you going
have little meaning anymore,
there's an endless darkened corridor
when you just need an open door.
You start to scream but there's just silence,
an empty hollow space,
thought the future had a meaning
but I'm walking out of pace.

Innocence

Whenever I feel lonely,
whenever I feel blue,
you bring me back to happiness
with the little things you do.
So small and frail, and innocent,
a special gift to me was sent.

In your hands you hold your toys,
in your eyes I see signs of pure joy,
I wish like you I could be,
so open and honest,
so innocent and free.

But you've given me a special joy,
so I dedicate this to you,
my baby boy.

True to your Self

Daughter, dream your dreams
and by just who you are,
follow all your hopes and wishes,
just don't go too far.
Take life by the hand and create your fantasies,
be all the things you want to be,
and sail on all the seas.
Never take just second best
and say... "I'll be that me,"
always have inside you
the person you can be!

A Simple Thanks

Through all my days of restlessness,
and all my years of selfishness,
you stood by me and saw it through;
during all the adversity you still stayed true.
I never gave you any thanks,
just carried on with those stupid pranks
never realising the hurt I'd caused,
in my way I never paused.

But now as I sit and think of the past,
I know only you were true to the last,
for when everyone else had left me for dead,
you still put my problems upon your head.
It's now that I realise there'd never be
a kinder friend in the world to me,
than the one that loved me above all others,
the kindest most caring of Gods dear mothers.

Lost Love the Bitterest of Pills

If I could speak to you, what would I say?
If you could answer, would it be to pray?
If I could look at you, what would you see?
If I was frightened, would you turn and comfort me?

The year is ending as a new one must begin,
so as you break a smile and clear your throat to sing,
and find a sherry with which to toast,
for a moment remember she who loved you most.
As now, with happy heart I bid a last farewell,
to a once important person...

Dear Dad, I knew him well!

Never Ending Circle

There may be at times at the moment
when our dreams seem on different paths,
when all the troubles we're facing
having taken the place of the laughs.
But always remember, that dreams come and go,
and problems subside in the end.
But one thing that is never faltering
is I need you, my partner, my friend!
So, whatever pathways await us,
be them good ones or bad,
as long as you're standing beside me,
my heart will always be glad.

The day that you held me beside you
and promised that your heart was mine
was the day I'll always remember,
a moment to cherish in time.

Silver Lining

There are often times when things go wrong,
and we start to feel we don't belong,
when all the joy has turned to sadness
and all the sanities to madness.
Caring seems a lost belief
when from sorrow there's no relief,
you feel that there's nowhere to turn
for in your soul the hatred burns.
But just when you feel there's nowhere to run
the clouds disappear and out comes the sun.

Auld Lang Syne

A glance on the street as you were walking past,
provokes the memory that will always last.
I saw your face; did you see mine?
That brief reflection lost in time.

So, a happy New Year I wish to you
when all tomorrows seemed bright and new.
All the best Dad, though we will never meet
for another Lang Syne interlinked to greet.

I will raise a glass every year to you
and cry a tear for the times we knew.

The World Stopped Caring

One day the world stopped caring
for people on the street,
forgot to say hello to the strangers they may meet.
We think the world is bad today
but tomorrow it gets worse
when everyone upon the planet gets the selfish curse.
So, look inside your backyard
and see what you can mend,
take every fellow being and treat him as a friend.

Don't hurt this world - it's hurt enough,
we don't need much more pain,
so accept that smile from a stranger
and let's all begin again.

A Quiet Plea

Blood flows through the veins,
cut it and watch it gush,
it's not the blue you've held,
but red that now will rush,
out of every pore of me,
seeping through my soul,
draining the inner part of me,
losing what was whole.

If I give myself will you ask a little more,
if I hide the sadness will you dig within the core?
Or will you just accept that I am fallible and weak,
walk beside the needing
and give the things they seek?

When I hold you closely it does not mean I am yours,
when I cry the tears it does not reflect the cause,
and when I say I'm lost,
only then will you be mine
and help me ease the pain within
and sip the human wine.

I used to laugh

I hurt so much,
the pain just can't be eased,
I want to smile,
but I just don't succeed.
I know I used to laugh,
but I can't remember how,
I had a passion,
but I can't find it now.
If my heart were heavier,
I think it would fall out.
If I didn't want to cry so much,
I think that I would shout!
There has to be a way
that I can bring back the smile,
that I can have a life again,
for at least a little while.
So lost, so scared,
so miserable,
so utterly alone.
Surrounded by so many
why am I on my own?
Dip inside my body
and resurrect my soul
make my heart beat stronger
mend the scars
and make me whole.
Help me learn the answers
help me find the way
and guide me towards
that brighter day.

The Shadow Beneath the Moon

I'll catch you someday soon
in the shadow of the moon,
for it's your voice and not your face
that cause the memory to race.
You're just a silhouette in time,
laughing words that once were mine,
but a brighter light you will be
inside the sadder part of me.
The future beckons me to come,
though the end has just begun.
Will I always seek the past,
the things of truth that never last.

You Made Me Want to Live

I remember thinking that I would die,
never see the tears that you would cry,
never feel you hold me tight again,
this time you couldn't remove the pain.
I always thought that death was ok,
the thing we all would do some day,
I didn't care when my time came,
it was just a part of life's big game.
But you change all that with just one touch,
I love you Simon so very much,
And the thought that our future was never to be
was the greatest pain in the world to me,
So when I awoke and saw your face
I thanked the Lord for the human race!
I now know how valuable a gift life is
and I cherish mine just for your kiss,
for all that we are and all that we'll be
I lived for you, please live for me.
And may our future go on and on
into old age, still happy and strong.

We All Get Burnt Someday

Your dreams hold me some place
I was never meant to be.
Wrapped themselves around
and tried to let my spirit free.
Resurrecting old emotion
in a whirlwind of desire,
illuminating feelings
in that never ending fire,
you scorched my fingers,
burnt my heart,
left an ember in my soul.
But, through the ashes of the lust,
the remnants of the fight,
there is still a spark
that lives to represent the night.

Our Place

When we met I felt closer to you
than I ever have to any human being,
your touch,
your eyes,
everything about you said that I could
love you forever.
There was never an ounce of doubt
that between us we could prevail
where everyone else had failed,
that we WERE that something.
That unit,
that strength
that no demons or no doubts could ever separate.
When I slept with you,
I slept on a cloud of contentment,
a safe place far away from the evils of life.
You were more than my partner,
you were my friend.
All of life's issues didn't matter,
wouldn't matter
and couldn't matter,
for you needed me wholly
and that was where I wanted to be.

Cocooned in a world that no one could penetrate,
our world,
where you found me every day and every night,
where we curled up together
when the world was getting too mean
for either of us to handle.
Where we could be ourselves
and individuals if we so wished,
no secrets and no lies,
a place of happiness,
unity, and peace.

Do you still remember that place?

Where is Hope?

Where is hope, it has to be here?
Somewhere is has to exist.
There cannot just be misery
there must be some joy here.
There has to be a way that I can find
a glistening light,
of hope eternal burning somewhere
deep within the night.
Guiding me toward it,
beckoning me to come,
asking for my light to join it.
Making us as one.

Somewhere there must be that light,
somewhere a way to smile,
a path that leads to happiness,
for it I'll walk that extra mile.
I've done the hurdles and broken every obstacle in
my way,
what more do I have to do?
to find a brighter day?

This life must have a rainbow
before it fades and dies;
it must have some sweet words to take
the bitterness off the lies.
It has to have a reason that's
beyond just hurt and pain,
for all the losses on the way
there has to be some gain.
If not, then life's a joke
and our existence just a farce.
If this is all there is to give,
then our maker is an arse.

Suicide is Painful

When you want to cry out,
but they won't hear your voice
what are you left with?
Where is the choice?
But as you decay,
can you feel the pain
of those that are living,
the ones that remain?
Are you now at peace?
Is the pain now a dream?
Is the ending all that it seemed?
Could I have helped?
Would you still be here?
Or is life just that one ultimate fear?

I wish you were living
I wish you were well,
but I hope you're now free
of your own personal hell.
I'm sorry, but I had another to love,
so may God care for you (or whatever's above)!

And I wish you peace as they lay you to rest,
for you didn't deserve this,
for failing life's test.

Good night, God Bless?

What's the Answer?

There are several ways that we can look at life,
the good, the bad,
the safe, the mad,
and the downright ridiculous.

We can shelter ourselves from failure,
by never taking risks,
prevent disappointment
by never expecting success,
accept second best...
It was a good life,
a safe life,
a BORING life,
but at least we never lost,
that is one way.

Or we can take a chance at life,
accept risk,
face danger,
try our luck.
Maybe we fail, maybe we succeed, but at least:
It was a mad life,
a different life,
it had its ups and downs,
but at least we gave life a CHANCE,
that's another way.

Scared and Confused

Lost and alone,
am feeling scared and confused,
a little bewildered
and very bemused
by all that I hear
and all that I see,
will anyone every really love me?
Distorted thank yous hide contorted lies,
false I love yous and tearless cries,
bigoted attitudes,
stereotype views.
I have the rhythm,
but they have the blues.
Can't win their battle,
so won't play the game.
They may have the weapons,
but I have the aim
and when it's all over
and love has been lost,
who'll pay the bill,
and will you count the cost?

Shades of Grey

No one notices all the demons
lying quietly in my head,
but when you're not looking,
they start to scream,
"I would be better off dead".
All the smiles and all the laughter
are just shrouds I learn to wear,
as I try to overcome the cross
that I can't bear.
Twisted thoughts run in to nightmares
and the dreams have lost their way,
all that once had colour
are now charcoal shades of grey.

The Mask

I wonder if you see through the mask that I wear
to the pain that has a hold on me,
I am living on the edge of a non-existent world
losing sight of reality.
If the demons are confusion, then the devil's desperation
and I'm lying near the edge of hell,
all the fears and the anguish,
disillusion and doubt,
would empty arms be waiting if I fell?
Can't visualise the future,
all the past is dead,
and todays just a way to exist,
there's got to be an answer,
there has to be a way,
if only I could see through the mist.

Let Me Fly

If you look in her eyes,
you'll see the dream she'll need,
the passion runs,
if you cut her, she'll bleed,
but if you hold her back then I'll suffocate.
I see heaven waiting to let me through the gate,
cos I can't go on like I am right now,
I don't know when and I'll never know how.
But, if I don't break free then I'll never have hope,
the rizzlers rolled but I ain't got the dope,
don't know where I'll find it or if I'll ever get high,
but though I love you deeply
can't you see I must fly?
And if I ever come home, will you still be there?
Will it really matter?
Do you even care?
So, when your bed is cold and the night is long,
will your love for me still be pure and strong?

United

Two hearts united as two souls learnt to fly,
my spirit soared but it didn't go too high
to get beyond all the pain and doubt,
no use in crying and I can't even shout.
The dream is ending but the feeling will still remain,
nothing ventured but nothing left to gain.

Hiding

There's more to me than meets the eye,
there's a part of me that can almost fly,
there's more to me than what you see,
cos baby, there's a lot more to me.

There's a devil woman burns deep inside,
a part of me I've just got to hide
until I feel the moments right
then I'll burst free and start to fight.

I'll hold my dream till it can come true,
till I've got the future well in view,
then I'll break free like a butterfly gliding free
and flying high weaving my name on a tapestry.

I'll be leaving a mark saying:
"This is me".

Not to Be

There's only so much we can take
until we see the big mistake,
so kiss me now and say you care
for when I turn around you won't be there.

We gave it love, we gave it dreams
but with different endings, different schemes.
Though we feel the desire within our heart
we will always still be worlds apart,
for though we dream with equal mind
we both have a different path to find.

I know the passion still has power
but I think we've seen our finest hour,
but no matter what you'll be my friend,
from the fiery start to the bitter end.

The Boundaries of Dreams

After all is said and done,
there will still be a battle for me to fight
for there's no such thing as happiness,
it's just a trickery in the night.
Contentment can only exist
within the boundaries of our dreams,
it cannot hold a value
in our ambitions and schemes.
And when reality has left us
with far too little to believe,
it's time to close the window,
lock the door and start to grieve,
for there's no room left
for the visions we had
in our childhood days,
the beautiful encounters
and pure souls
we saw in plays.

Fortress of Sadness

On the top of a mountain
standing tall and alone,
rigid and lifeless
as the wind around doth moan,
is the castle of hatred,
the prison of sin,
in the fortress of sadness,
the lonely give in.

Its molasses covered stonework
hides cold labyrinths carved in hate.
It's only link to freedom
is an awesome steel caste gate.
A thousand tears have laid to rest
upon its concrete floors,
as soldiers of the fortress
slam closed its lifeless doors.

Now shrouded in the veil of black,
the grey and white march on,
the lives and loves that they once knew
are for the moment gone.
So, if you should pass its cold black gaze,
be grateful you are free,
And spare a thought for those brave souls
that gave their lives for thee.

Forgotten Laughter

Burning visions of a childhood now that's past.
Twisted memories of a time that couldn't last.
Forgotten laughter now lays muffled in pain,
as those sunny days gave way to all the rain.
The words are more staccato
as the meaning lost its lust,
for all that we once were is now blown away
like dust,
like pebbles on a beach that shimmered in the day,
just like those fragile stones,
our lives were washed away.
The union of two spirits cannot outlive the change,
no matter what the dreams
or how remote the range.
But, when you look into the sky,
you'll see a star that's me,
the one that stands for yesterday
and dreams that cannot be.

Bedlam - 1991

What's going off in my brain?
Am I verging on insane?
The voices they call out to me,
through the cloak of sanity,
crying freedom in my ears
and sadness through my tears.

The harder I try to hold on,
the more I find my strength has gone.
My will to live, my want to be,
are slipping away from me.
I shout aloud and make a noise,
but no one seems to hear my voice.

I can't find words to say how I feel.
The meanings lost; the words unreal.
Can't you see I'm falling fast,
the fight in me has long since passed.
Right or wrong, good or bad,
am I sane or simply mad?

Friend or Foe?

You're a difficult man to comprehend,
are you an enemy or a friend?
Or is it a simple clash of personality?
Do you find it so hard to understand me?
Why can't we talk in a civilised tongue,
instead of trying to prove me wrong?
Talk to me for a little while
and you might begin to like my style.

We're not as different as we might seem,
for we both plot, and we both scheme,
of how we'd like the world to be,
if you looked, you'd see yourself in me.
Younger and less qualified,
but just as stubborn and dignified.

Don't fight me, but help me to understand,
don't give me your fist but your open hand.
Just give me your friendship is all I ask,
is this request so hard a task?

The Final Farewell

What the hell is going off?
I don't know where I am, I'm lost
inside your sorrow.
When you play the big 'I am',
if I could, I'd be that little woman that you need, but I can't cos
I am arrogant
and of a different breed.

Anger take it's hold,
of that there is no doubt,
but there are times when clear of mind
I still will scream and shout.
And that's because I love you,
though God knows I should not,
for all that I have been to you
you simply have forgot.

So place your arms on someone else
and let them feel my fear,
for I will not stay anymore
I've had enough my dear.

My Sweet Little Boy

My sweet little boy asleep in your bed,
happy and contented with dreams in your head.
We've had our problems you and I,
but we trudged on and we got by.
We shared the laughter and the tears,
and together we've fought our greatest fears.
A perfect duo were we two,
for you had me and I had you.

So, no matter what the future holds,
in to what kind of man you finally mould.
You will always be my dearest treasure,
for you were my hope
and you brought me pleasure.

Another World

Ever wanted to escape?
Then walk to toward the screen
and leave this black and painful world behind.
Your fingers dance like angels upon the cold grey keys,
lost, devoid of realism, another world you find.

I ask the question once again.
And then the answer comes...
Now I can be whoever,
there are no boundaries here,
no face, no body, only me,
whoever that may be.
The person infinite,
I'm powerful, without fear.

For then I'm lost within myself,
so great I am, so fine.
Whatever you may wish of me,
is that which you will find.

A Rainbow of Roses

What is a dream?
It's the rainbow we hold in our hands,
the unthinkable possession,
the untouchable pot of gold,
the thing we all admire,
adore and desire.

To hold the true gift of light in your fingertips,
that is but a dream.
But we can hold life,
love and ambition,
cherish it,
cuddle it,
live for it
and at times die for it.

What is hope?
Like the rose that stands proud and beautiful,
depicting all that man desires, gives and promises.
In the daylight it holds its head high as if to say:
"I am special, I am perfect,
I AM LOVE".

In the evening as the darkness falls
it is still a beautiful rose,
depicting all that we be even as the light fades
over its beauty
and our lives.

The Mirror Never Lies

Harmonious reflection
looking back through tinted glass
smile with vague remembrance
of a time forever passed.

We walked a thousand miles
within the reflection I now see,
and yet there is no part of you
that resembles any part of me.

If we travel deeper,
will we again become as one
or is the distance travelled
too great to overcome?

So, all I ask is we reflect
on the things we both have been,
all that we once were
and all that I have seen.

Canvas of Blood

Screamed at the world,
it screamed right back at me,
Saw the master but he
would not let me be free.
The barrier is broken,
the heart is torn apart.
I saw the picture
and they called it modern art,
a scrambled mess of paint
against the canvas we call it,
where artists use a brush,
he used a pointed knife.
Red was the colour
the canvas held so well,
Silence was the voice
that truth will never tell.
Black was the heart
from which the painting grew,
and lost was the memory,
the subtlest of hews.

Deceived

Contorted reflections of feelings that died,
twisted by hatred, knowing that you lied.
Sweet memories, drowning in all of my pain,
gasp for survival. Their fight is in vain.

Don't try to rekindle the flame that is dead,
to me you're a book that I've finished and read,
don't wish to go over the same old line,
you're now a dark memory... the future is mine.

Forbidden Fruit

You are the man that made me feel
more than I ever thought I could,
took me to the sort of places
I never thought I should,
taught me to believe
in the woman that I am
and made me see the difference
between a child and a man.
You are all the man
I ever want and ever need,
and if that is avarice
then give me some more greed!
Hold me in your loving arms
and never let me go...
Take me to another world
where only we two know.
And on that special day,
look into my eyes
and see that there could never be
between us any lies.
That you will always be
the very one for me:
My life... my love... my future...
The one that set me free.

Reasons to Smile

When we wake up in the morning
to the sun shining back.
When your best friend wags
their tail and says hello.
When today's pains disappear,
and we find tomorrows dreams.
When someone we care for
just rings to say hello.
When the person that we love
makes breakfast just because.
When Mother's Day is remembered
by a daughter or a son.

For just one moment we become a special someone.

The Two of Us

I dreamed a dream of you one day
in a garden where the two of us would play.
Fairies danced as we chased demons out of sight,
lived for the moment, and took our dreams into the night.

Then we held hands on a playground full of pain,
held on so tightly when the devil called our names.
Now we're still those children but fighting without end.
The spirits may be lost in time,
but the memories make us friends.

A Bygone Age

She sits alone in her rocking chair,
with wrinkled face and greying hair,
although her hands are twisted
and her feet are taut and blistered,
she does not hold any grudges
as over the years her faith never budges.

Although her body's seen better days,
her mind and soul still bright and gay.
For she's the daughter of a better age,
she's a leaf off a different page.
Always caring for the needs of others,
she is one of life's Great Grandmothers.

The Man on the Hill

His heart is kind,
but his words are cruel,
in his mind he feels the fool.
The world to him
is a sorrowful place,
and his outlook is dim
for the human race.

Try as he may
to understand,
he will always stay part
of a forgotten land.
Black and white,
to him don't go,
he can't see the light,
he just doesn't know.

For my Daughter on her Wedding Day

Diddly, I never thought the day would come,
when I would see you as a bride,
although you always know it will happen,
that the time would soon arrive.
So now that we are here on the eve of your wedding day,
there are a few choice words your Mum would like to say:

Remember, although you'll become a wife,
you're still little 'Dids' for the rest of your life.
And, if you ever need me, I'll always be here,
whether mending the pain, or helping you cheer!
And there'll be nobody prouder tomorrow at Two,
than this silly woman who gave birth to you.

So good health and happiness my special girl,
may a wonderful life for you unfurl.

Desperation

People say it's just a hiccup,
but you know it's something more.
Hold the knife and watch the blade shine...
Is life still worth fighting for?

One simple slash and its oblivion.
No pain for you to feel,
then is suicide just a cop out,
or a way that we can heal?

The pain keeps turning in your head,
and the screws are getting tight.
The cogs have lost their thread
and your will has lost its fight.

When the time comes to say it's over,
have you anywhere to go?
For you can't find that four leaf clover
or take another blow.

So as tears fall upon the gravestone
remember I'm at rest.
At last, I'm free from sorrow though,
forever flown the nest.

Ended

"I'm lost"...
        "So am I".

"Where's the dream?"...
        "I'm sorry but it died".

"Where's the future?"
        "There isn't one, I lied".

"So, where's the hope?"...
        "Left drowning with your fears".

"And my fantasies?"...
        "They're left to mingle with your tears".

In the following section you will find a small number of poems taken from scribblings on the pages, half found poems, thoughts in ink added almost as an afterthought - on the backs of other poems, as if inspired by the poets own words; furious writing showing the passion and need to get the words out.

Here lie the echoes of a different kind of creation. These are the poems born on the backside of dreams, the whispers of thought jotted down on the margins of life. They are the after thoughts, the sudden sparks, the whispers of the muse before she's fully formed them.

Don't expect grand pronouncements or perfect lines. Find instead the raw edges of inspiration, the fleeting moments captured in a hurried scrawl. Let these scraps and scribbles invite you into the messy, beautiful process of creation, where even the smallest spark can ignite a fire.

Katy Streets

Life Foundations

We often have chance meetings,
or expect circumstances to last forever.

It is only later and often in the quiet of the night
when the only sound is our own heartbeat,
that we realise just how fragile life is
and how much someone has touched our lives.

Untitled #1

Grasping at straws in the morning light
with hope,
with smiles,
with hearts so strong
they will see this through and be loyal.

Confused, bewildered.
Lost & scared,
But is anybody there?

Untitled #2

So, what is life when you think about it?
The ins and outs,
the what's, the ifs,
the in-betweens,
the should we,
would we, could be's.

Maybe it is about the bits in between:
The no monies,
no fuel,
no baths tonight.

A fire,
a mattress,
a cuddle tight.

Untitled #3

No comfort in three under the same roof.
The look you give is the very proof.
The one you want is the one you smile with,
but brutal hurt to her you give,
and your heart still lives inside.

Oh, you're hurting,
still hurting.
Oh bugger,
JUST CRY.

Untitled #4

There is no such thing as perfection.
Promises hurt and break you.
Sisters sit in judgement.
Fathers tell the words.
People manipulate you,
and only you will hurt.
Reality, oh they can bring it on,
but at the end,
behind closed doors,
you break.

Half Discovered

.....
But still you hurl the stones and cut me quick,
defamate my character
and disrespect my right to have a mind that understands,
and isn't purely thick,
to have the strength to carry on,
to stand up tall and fight.

For I am a woman through and through,
in every little pore burns the desire to succeed,
with dignity and respect.
I have no need to tell you what my actions may be for,
no need to skulk in corners or run away and hide.

So look at me and see the determination that I hold,
the knowledge that I'll be someone before I'm very old.

Printed in Great Britain
by Amazon